ADVENTURES

In Your National Parks

SCREAMING WITH EXCITEMENT, *park visitor Amanda Peet rides rapids on the Colorado River in Arizona's Grand Canyon.*

JAMES BALOG

COVER: *At Yosemite National Park, in California, Louis Poimiroo, 10, practices techniques of rock climbing.*

GALEN ROWELL

□ BOOKS FOR WORLD EXPLORERS
□ NATIONAL GEOGRAPHIC SOCIETY

CONTENTS

*Hundreds of Parks,
Countless Adventures 3*

Copyright © 1988 National Geographic Society
Library of Congress CIP data: page 96

MOUNTAIN PEAKS AND THICK FOREST *frame Lake O'Hara in Canada's Yoho National Park, in British Columbia.*

HUNDREDS OF PARKS, COUNTLESS ADVENTURES

Where can you climb some of the oldest mountains on earth, explore a glacier, and snorkel among tropical fish? The ideal vacation isn't in any one spot. But these experiences—and many more— await you in the national parks of the United States and Canada.

The U. S. National Park Service oversees facilities—nearly 350 of them—in every region of the country. Parks Canada offers recreation in 32 parks scattered coast to coast. Of the U. S. areas, 49 are national parks in the strictest sense. The rest include seashores, old battlefields, and scenic trails and riverways.

National parks exist to preserve the natural heritage and to make it available to everyone. The task is not easy. The park services rely on the public to help by following park rules. Millions of people visit the parks every year. They are asked to take out what they bring in, and nothing more. There's no picking of wildflowers, and no taking of any other natural souvenirs. That would mar the beauty for other visitors—like you. And people are asked not to feed any animals they come across. It's a matter both of preservation and of safety.

The main parks featured in this book are seven among many. They represent the wide range of facilities available to you.

Yellowstone National Park, which is mostly in Wyoming, pulses with the world's greatest concentration of geysers, hot pools, and other thermal features. Puffs of steam fill the sky the year round. A visit to Yellowstone will place you in the oldest national park in the world.

Everglades National Park, in Florida, has the largest subtropical wilderness in the United States. The park was created to preserve not only its scenery but also its delicate balance of plant and animal life. To fully appreciate the Everglades, take your time. You might want to see it from a canoe, getting an alligator's-eye view.

3

NATIONAL GEOGRAPHIC PHOTOGRAPHER JAMES P. BLAIR

HIKERS TACKLE A WILDERNESS TRAIL *in Great Smoky Mountains National Park in North Carolina. Though the park is the most heavily visited in the United States, it's easy to get away from the crowd. Just ask a ranger to point you to the kind of trail you want to follow. Rangers are pleased to help.*

President Theodore Roosevelt once called Yosemite National Park, in California, "the most beautiful place on earth." At Yosemite, giant sequoias seem to scrape the sky. The nation's highest waterfalls tumble from sheer cliffs. Bare granite mountain faces dare the brave to climb.

Towering dunes greet bicyclers at Cape Cod National Seashore, in Massachusetts. Miles of paved trails allow smooth pedaling alongside often rough seas. Visitors learn it was the treachery of those seas that forced the Pilgrims to land on the cape, north of their destination.

In Canada's Pacific Rim National Park, in British Columbia, tangled forests slope to the thundering surf. Black bears lumber through the wilderness. Offshore, migrating whales glide through the sea. Kayakers come across sea lions resting on rocky islands.

Hikers in Oregon's Crater Lake National Park see a magnificent sight. The lake is like a great blue sapphire ringed by an emerald forest. Deepest in the United States, the lake was born of volcanic activity. Visitors can see deep into its dark blue waters.

You may choose to visit the Grand Canyon, in Arizona. One of the best ways to experience this spectacular national park is from the bucking seat of a rubber boat bounding down the Colorado River. If you climb the canyon walls, you'll see two billion years of the earth's history revealed in the rocks.

No matter which park you visit, you'll enjoy it more if you have time to linger. Of course, you can see the important sights from the passenger seat of a car, but you'll miss a lot. If you prepare thoughtfully, your only problem during a park visit may be deciding if you're having too good a time. Here are some tips to help you.

• Write to the park you've chosen well in advance. Make sure the park is open when you want to visit. Ask for a map of the park and for information on recreational activities.

JUMPING INTO A PARK EXPERIENCE. *At a cooling-off spot in Grand Canyon National Park, in Arizona, a visitor gets set for splashdown.*

• Compare the costs and benefits of camping with those of staying in a lodge or hotel. Check whether reservations are needed for lodging and for park activities.

• To avoid the crowds, think about making your trip off-season—in most cases, spring, fall, or winter. As an alternative, consider visiting a lesser known park.

• Pack carefully. Consider the weather expected for the time of year. Think about the activities in which you will be taking part.

• Leave your pet with a sitter. Though some parks allow pets on a leash, they can interfere with your pleasure and with the enjoyment of others.

Remember the activities mentioned at the beginning of this introduction? You'll find them, in order, at Great Smoky Mountains National Park, North Carolina and Tennessee; Glacier National Park, Montana; and Buck Island Reef National Monument, St. Croix, in the U. S. Virgin Islands.

AT A GLANCE . . .

In a hurry? Each chapter of this book contains a section called "At a Glance . . . ." A few brief paragraphs provide helpful background and visitor information, including an address to write for more information. Symbols give a quick summary of the main activities the park offers. The symbols, with their meanings, are—

 Backpacking or hiking.

 Bicycling.

 Boating. Check for restrictions on types of boats.

 Camping. Check for types of facilities available.

 Climbing. May require special equipment.

 Fishing.

 Riding—horseback or burro.

 Skiing.

 Swimming.

5

1 | Skiing Through YELLOWSTONE

Days earlier, a herd of wild bison blazed the trail. Now four young skiers glide along it, enjoying the dazzling wintry wilderness of Yellowstone National Park. The world's oldest national park, Yellowstone offers adventure to visitors the year round.

'There is something in the wild romantic scenery of this valley which I cannot . . . describe. . . .'
—Trapper Osborne Russel, about 1830

Four young cross-country skiers glide through a wintry world of snow-covered meadows and evergreens glistening with ice. They stop to watch an unforgettable sight, a giant jet of steam and water that can shoot as high as a 20-story building.

That jet of water is doubtless the most famous geyser in the world—Old Faithful. It is one of more than 200 geysers in Yellowstone National Park. The park lies in a volcanic area. A few thousand feet below the surface, melted rock called magma heats rock layers above. The rock layers in turn heat water that has seeped underground. Pressure builds, and the geysers erupt. The underground heat also creates the park's 10,000 other thermal features: hot springs, bubbling mudpots, and hissing fountains of steam.

The park brims with "firsts" and "mosts." Founded in 1872, Yellowstone is the oldest national park in the world—and one of the largest. Rhode Island and Delaware would fit inside it with room to spare. It sprawls over parts of three states: Wyoming, Montana, and Idaho. It holds the largest mountain lake in North America. And Yellowstone may have the largest concentration of large and small mammals in the United States outside Alaska.

Sixteen-year-old Emma Fuller and her sister, Skye, 14, live in the heart of Yellowstone, at Canyon Village, Wyoming. Erin McClure, 14, and her brother, Gavin, 11, live in Gardiner, Montana, just outside the park. Together with Erin and Gavin's parents, the four strapped on skis and set out to explore Yellowstone.

The Fullers and the McClures have learned to live with the heavy snows that cover Yellowstone for five months of the year. When snow closes the roads to automobile traffic, Skye and Emma travel some of the 40 miles to school by snowmobile. To Yellowstone natives, cross-country skiing is not only an enjoyable activity, but also one of the best ways to see the park in winter.

Skye has been cross-country skiing almost

YELLOWSTONE NATIONAL PARK

Winter sunrise at Yellowstone

Like some mountain spirit, a frost halo shimmers around a tree growing from a rocky cliff. Halos like this one appear only in the morning in sub-zero weather. They form as thermal steam rises and freezes. The resulting ice crystals stay suspended in the air. They seem to glow as rays from the low-lying sun shine through them. Scenes like this one draw about a hundred thousand wintertime visitors to Yellowstone. Throughout the year about two and a third million people visit the park.

9

> **'The snow was perfect. There was powder on top. It was great for going down hills.'**
>
> —Emma Fuller, 16

since she could walk. "My parents used to carry me on their backs when I was very little," she says. "Then I learned to ski by myself when I was 2 or 3. We all have several pairs of skis."

"Skiing is a lot of fun," says Emma. "We go most weekends." The skiers outfit themselves with caps, boots, wool sweaters, warm pants, and sunglasses. "You always have to wear sunglasses," Emma cautions. "The sunlight reflects off the snow; it can produce a painful glare if your eyes aren't protected."

On a crisp December morning, the group set out for the lower region of the park. That's where Old Faithful and other *(Continued on page 16)*

Whoops!

Erin McClure, on top, and Skye Fuller, both 14, take a tumble at the base of a hill but come up smiling. "We did a lot of those!" says Skye. "We fell a lot because both of us like to ski down big hills really fast." Skye lives inside the park, at Canyon Village, Wyoming. Erin lives in nearby Gardiner, Montana.

Downhill racer

His gaze set on the course ahead, Erin's brother, Gavin, 11, skims straight down a slope. On a steeper hill, he might zigzag down for greater control. The steamy mist in the background comes from hot springs and from fumaroles (FYOO-muh-roles)— *vents in the earth that release steam but not water. Yellowstone is the most active thermal area in the world. Its hot springs, fumaroles, geysers, and boiling mudpots number about 10,000 in all.*

Old Faithful, undoubtedly the world's most famous geyser, sends a plume of steam and water high into the crisp December sky. The four adventurers rest on their ski poles as they take in the view. Old Faithful erupts predictably about once every 80 minutes—thus its name. In 1988, raging fires came close to Old Faithful. The fires destroyed hundreds of square miles of forest before early fall snows helped bring them under control. Over many years, the charred areas should grow back green, thick, and healthy.

Taking the plunge

Gavin gets set to jump into hot-water runoff from Boiling River, where an icy stream and thermal waters mix. The result: bathing luxury fit for a king!

Thermal features

Below the earth's surface, at varying depths, lie pockets of melted rock called magma. The magma heats the rock layers above it. In thermal areas like Yellowstone, surface water seeps down through porous, or sponge-like, rock. As it reaches the hot rock, the water is heated. It rises back to the surface, creating hot springs, fumaroles, mudpots, and geysers.

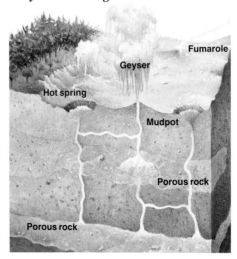

Fumarole

Geyser

Hot spring

Mudpot

Porous rock

Porous rock

14

After-ski relaxation

Erin, left, and Skye bathe in Boiling River hot-water runoff. The girls wear caps to keep their hair from freezing after they leave the water. Heat from the water melts snow that falls along the banks. The heat promotes the growth of various kinds of plants along the river's edges. Boiling River is one of only two hot-water areas where bathing is permitted. Rangers monitor both places for safety.

Making tracks

A pine marten pauses for an instant as it hunts for food in the snow (left). Pine martens, which are related to weasels, grow about two feet long. "We see them all the time," says Skye. "They like to play tricks. They go in little holes and peek out. They jump up on the window sill and look in at our cats."

Facing bad weather

Nose toward the wind, a bull elk stands alert during a snowstorm (opposite). Elk are the most common large animal in Yellowstone; the herd numbers about 20,000. The park may have the largest concentration of large and small mammals in the United States outside Alaska.

JAMES H. ROBINSON

 AT A GLANCE . . .

Yellowstone offers spectacular scenery and a variety of things to do. (Temporary restrictions on some park activities may be in effect as a result of the fires of 1988.) Yellowstone is open year-round, though in winter many roads are closed by snow. The winter season ordinarily lasts from October 31 to May 1. Though automobile traffic is restricted, snowmobiles are permitted. You can also see the park from motor coaches run by private companies.

A road system in the shape of a figure eight takes you to the park's main attractions. In addition to Old Faithful, these include Mammoth Hot Springs, the Grand Canyon of the Yellowstone, and Yellowstone Lake. Here fishing and boating are permitted.

A thousand miles of trails and more than two thousand campsites promise plenty of rugged adventure. Be sure to check with rangers on trail and weather conditions. Feeding of bears is strictly prohibited. Keep your distance from *all* animals in the park.

For more information write—
Superintendent, Yellowstone
National Park, WY   82190

(Continued from page 10) geysers are concentrated. The trip took the skiers through forest and meadow and over rolling hills. The hills are tiresome to climb, but whisking down is always a thrill. "Erin and I like to ski down the hills really fast," says Skye. "We often go at the same time—and bump into each other and end up in a pile at the bottom of the hill. We break up laughing."

When the skiers finally reached Old Faithful, the air was cold and sparkling clear—ideal for viewing the geyser. "It was dramatic!" says Erin. "We seemed close enough to touch it." (Spectators are kept a safe distance from the scalding water.) "First there's a lot of steam," Erin continues. "Next you hear a roar. Then the water spews high into the air. It lasts only a couple of minutes, but it's a sight you never forget."

Old Faithful spouts on schedule about once every 80 minutes. It has done so at least since people started keeping track of it more than 120 years ago. The first frontiersmen to see the thermal features were trappers. They entered Yellowstone in the early part of the 19th century. Gold miners followed in the 1860s. Word of the mysterious hot pools and spouting waters spread around the world. People wondered: Were the stories

Furry snowplow

Searching for grass, a bison pushes away snow with its muzzle. At 2,000 pounds top weight, the bison is the largest animal in the park. Despite their weight, bison can move surprisingly fast—up to 30 miles an hour.

'O'er the fields we go . . . '

On a trek by snowmobile, Skye (in front, right), Emma, and Erin pause near a herd of bison. Once, there were as many as 60 million bison, but they were hunted almost to extinction in the United States in the 1800s. Today in the U. S. there are more than 40,000 bison in parks, preserves, and ranches.

true—or just tall tales spun out over campfires by imaginative backwoodsmen?

In 1871 a survey team went to Yellowstone to find out. It brought out photographs as proof of the area's splendors. Convinced that Yellowstone was indeed special, Congress drew up a bill to set the area aside for protection. On March 1, 1872, President Ulysses S. Grant signed the bill into law, creating Yellowstone National Park.

In its early years, Yellowstone was a park in name only. The whole idea was new, and Congress didn't quite know how to set up a national park. The superintendent had no money to run the huge

area he had been put in charge of. Squatters—illegal settlers—moved in. Hunters and trappers killed wildlife. One observer wrote: "[Visitors came] with shovel and axe, chopping and hacking and prying up great pieces of the most ornamental work [natural rock formations] they could find." Finally, in 1886, the U. S. Cavalry was put in control of Yellowstone.

In the following years, other wild and scenic areas, including Crater Lake and Yosemite, were set aside as national parks. It became apparent that a special agency was needed to run them. In 1916, Congress established the National Park Service. Its

A landscape in constant change

An ice cone the size of a house has built up around one of Yellowstone's 200 geysers. This geyser was inactive for many years, then suddenly resumed activity. The forces below the surface are unpredictable. Surprises appear every year.

mission: to preserve and protect park areas for the enjoyment of all the people.

The park's thermal area provides habitats for a variety of animals during the harsh winter. Visitors may see bison, mule deer, swans, and geese. They might even spot an elk or a rare bald eagle—or a moose. Emma makes a habit of hanging her ski poles from a tree when she's through skiing. "That way the moose won't get at them," she says. "They like to eat the leather handles."

Even in winter the temperature of Yellowstone's hot springs holds steady at around 200°F. That's hot enough to poach an egg. Green plants sprout along the edges of hot springs and runoff areas. Insects skim along steamy surfaces. If they stray more than a few inches from the heat, they freeze instantly.

In a few places, hot springs flow into cold rivers. That can make the water just right for bathing. "It's relaxing to take a hot-springs bath after skiing," says Erin. "I like to be right in the middle. If you're too far on one side, it's too hot. If you're too far on the other, it's too cold."

"Bathing is a lot of fun when it's cold and snowy," says Emma. "The hot water turns your skin raspberry. When you get out, you have to bundle yourself up right away."

Only two places in the park are open to bathers. They are closely monitored by rangers. "What's safe one year is not necessarily safe the next," says Roderick Hutchinson, a geologist at Yellowstone. "Unseen forces inside the earth create these features—and change them. A pleasantly warm bathing spring this year might be icy cold or boiling hot the next. Steam vents and mudpots appear and disappear. Geysers come and go."

Geysers come and go? What about Old Faithful? Might it dry up? "The fact is, we just don't know for sure," says Hutchinson. "Old Faithful could stop spouting tomorrow." He pauses a moment and smiles. "But I have a hunch she'll be around for a long, long time to come."

2 | Watery World Of the EVERGLADES

Surrounded by cypress trees, ranger Isobel Kalafarski and a group of Miami sixth graders explore a wetland trail in Big Cypress National Preserve, alongside Everglades National Park. They use walking sticks to feel for holes. With luck, the youngsters may spot some rare forms of Florida wildlife along the way.

'In this park ... we shall protect hundreds of kinds of wildlife which might otherwise soon be extinct.'

—President Harry S. Truman
at dedication of Everglades National Park, 1947

Less than an hour's drive from one of the busiest and fastest growing cities in the United States there lies a vast wilderness. It is a wetland that has open prairies, mangrove swamps, saltwater marshes, and freshwater lakes. The area shelters a large variety of animals, including many that are rare and endangered.

This wilderness is Everglades National Park. It is the largest subtropical wilderness in the United States. The park takes up an area about the size of Delaware and covers much of the southern tip of Florida. Lying just 35 miles west of Miami, it is convenient to large numbers of people.

Once, only a relatively small number of Native Americans, or Indians, inhabited the region. One group, the Miccosukee, called the area Pahayokee (pah-HIGH-oh-kee)—"waters of grass." Grasses are a symbol of the Glades. More than a hundred kinds grow there.

It was the British, though, who gave the area its present name. They controlled Florida from 1763 to 1783, after taking it from Spain in a war. The British observed that the wetland resembled an everlasting glade, or open meadow. Ever since, the area has been called the Everglades.

Visitors say taking your time is the key to enjoying the Everglades. "You need to develop a sharp eye to really appreciate the park," says 10-year-old Kimberly Hutchison. "If you don't pay attention, you could miss a lot of things."

The landscape may seem monotonous to a first-time visitor. Actually, the scenery holds many surprises. "There are hundreds of things right in front of your eyes," says Kimberly. "You just have to look carefully. I've seen baby alligators swimming in the water, big alligators hiding in the grass, and anhingas [a kind of bird] blending into the trees."

Kimberly visited the park as part of a school program. Every year, the park welcomes thousands of students. Many of them come from Miami, as do all the adventurers in this chapter.

The best ways to see the park are by canoe

24

Wet wilderness

Taking advantage of a watery highway, canoeists in Everglades National Park paddle through a mangrove swamp. Mangrove trees grow in warm coastal areas. They have roots that stick out of the water like a jumble of stilts. The park, which makes up one-seventh of the entire Everglades region, lies at the southern tip of Florida. Farming and the growth of cities have destroyed much of the Everglades outside the park. The park provides a haven for many rare and endangered animals.

EVERGLADES NATIONAL PARK

GEORG GERSTER

Water, water . . . everywhere?

A special map helps ranger Ann Deutch demonstrate southern Florida's water system — and water problems (right). All the region's fresh water comes from rains. Much of the water seeps underground, trickling to the Biscayne aquifer (yellow sponge). The aquifer is a natural underground reservoir consisting of rock that holds water like a sponge. It is from the aquifer that Miami and other cities get their water. In time there may not be enough to go around. More and more people are moving into southern Florida. They need water. Farmers need it. So do factories. And certainly the Everglades does. Finding ways to meet the needs of all will require inventiveness and wisdom. Here, Kimberly Hutchison, left, and Susie Somoza, both 10, hold the map as ranger Deutch pours the "rainfall." "When we waste water," says Deutch, "it's like taking it from the alligators."

and on foot. Hiking at night is especially popular. "It was really dark," says Dawn Roig, 11, of a night hike she took with classmates. "The woods seemed to close in around you. Animals came out of their dens and nests to feed, to drink water, and to hunt. They hardly made a sound. The Glades are so quiet at night."

Dawn's group went canoeing, too. Many of the students had never been in a canoe, much less navigated one. Before they came to the park, they practiced paddling at school, using brooms. By the time they got to the Everglades, they were ready to use their newly found skills by going on a scavenger hunt on a lake.

The students had to collect a list of natural items—on paper. They didn't actually gather up anything, but made a note when they spotted something on the list. Among the items: cattails, sawgrass, turtles—and alligators.

"I'd never been on a lake with alligators in it," says Stephanie Noel, 11. "On the scavenger hunt,

Canoe with a view

For many visitors, canoeing is the only way to go (left). It gives them a chance to see the park close up, from its natural element, water. The park has programs for school groups ranging from one-day visits to four-day camp-outs. Youngsters go on scavenger hunts by canoe. They take hikes at night, when many animals are most active. They examine animal life in swamps. They camp on dry mounds called hammocks, sleeping in tents.

Left, then right, then left . . .

New to canoeing, Stephanie Noel, 11, gets a feel for the paddle. "One day," she says, "we went out before the sun rose and listened to all the sounds of early morning—fish splashing, birds singing. It was so beautiful!" Stephanie lives in Miami, as do the other youngsters in this chapter.

I got close to some alligators—but not too close!" Alligators are fast when they're hungry, and they'll eat just about anything.

Alligators play a vital role in the fragile cycle that keeps the Everglades alive. In winter months—the dry season—some areas of the park dry up. Water remains only in ponds and in existing holes that have been cleaned out and deepened by alligators. Fish, turtles, snails, and other creatures seek out these "gator holes" for survival. The oases in turn attract larger animals searching for food. When the rains come, the survivors—both predators and prey—return to their normal habitats. The alligator's role in the cycle has earned it the title "keeper of the Everglades."

The Everglades is actually a river—a very unusual river. It's about 100 miles long, 50 miles wide, and (on average) 9 inches deep. It flows from Lake Okeechobee southward to the Gulf of Mexico.

The current is so slow that it's measured in inches per day rather than in feet per second—the usual way of measuring river flow.

Water is the area's lifeblood. Without water, the Everglades would die. But demand for that water is increasing. Farmers need it for crops. Expanding cities need it for drinking and for public facilities such as swimming pools. Cities need it for sewage removal. Manufacturers use huge amounts of water in turning out their products.

In wet years, there's generally enough to go around. In dry years, disputes arise. Who gets the water—the people or the park? So far, the park, aided by its supporters, has managed to hang on. But as the population of southern Florida grows, so does the problem of water management.

What better way to learn about water than by jumping right in? Adventurers do just that on a slough slog. A slough (SLOO) is a swamp. It supports a large variety of plant and animal life.

Ranger Isobel Kalafarski leads students on slough slogs in a section of the Everglades called Big Cypress National Preserve. The "uniform" is long pants and sneakers. "We give sloggers a pole. It's like a third leg," says Kalafarski. "We give them a hand lens, which is like a third eye."

Hikers dip small nets into the water. They put the creatures they find into a pail. The hikers examine the creatures before returning them to the water. "You don't do this in any other park I know of," Kalafarski says. "Youngsters can see firsthand how the little animals in the water are important to the bigger animals."

Some sloggers are a little afraid at first about entering the slough. "They may have seen scary jungle movies showing alligators, wild cats, and poisonous snakes," says the ranger. "Actually, most of these animals avoid humans." Sloggers who do have fears to begin with usually lose them once they've been in the water a few minutes.

For many visitors, like Samuel Lonaix, the slog is a high point of a *(Continued on page 32)*

'What have we got here?'

Peering into his dip net, Samuel Lonaix examines his catch. With schoolmates, Samuel hiked through a slough in Big Cypress National Preserve, next to the park. The students swished nets through the water, catching glass shrimp, tiny snails, and other creatures. They learned that the small forms of life are eaten by bigger animals. "Having a supply of food and water—that's one of the most important things in nature," Samuel observes.

Crayfish encounter

Pedro Colón, 12, examines a crayfish found during the slough slog (above). Crayfish look like miniature versions of their relative the lobster. They have claws that they use for holding prey. This crayfish didn't use its claws on the person holding it. "It was trying to crawl away," Pedro says.

Fishing from the pad-io

A colorful bird called a common moorhen stands on a lily pad. Its large, spread-out feet seem perfectly suited to the perch. From the pad, the bird catches small fish.

DOUGLAS GRUENAU

Wildlife trail

At a viewing station along the Anhinga Trail, Mark Philogene, 12, points something out to his friend Loubens Jean-Louis, also 12 (above). The popular trail winds through one of the heaviest concentrations of wildlife in the park. Sawgrass, the tooth-edged plants seen here, covers much of the Everglades.

In the pink

Wings flapping, a roseate spoonbill comes in for a graceful landing on a park pond. The bird's diet of shrimp helps give it its pink color. Dozens of kinds of birds numbering in the millions find shelter in the park.

'At the zoo, you see animals in enclosures. The Everglades is better.'

—Loubens Jean-Louis, 12

Look—but don't touch

Prickly spines on its stem make the bull thistle a treat for eyes only. Flowers bloom year-round here, each kind in its own time.

'Keeper of the Everglades'

That's the nickname this fearsome predator has made for itself. The alligator plays an essential role in the fragile cycle of life in the Everglades. Only two seasons come to the area: wet and dry. During the wet season, alligators root around in mudholes and in deep spots underwater. That cleans the holes out and makes them deeper. During the dry season, the holes retain water when almost everything else is parched. Animals large and small, predators and prey, flock to the holes. In this indirect way, the gators provide the animals with water, food, and a chance of survival. When the rains come, the survivors scatter once again to their habitats throughout the Glades.

Rare sight

A Florida panther perches in a bald cypress in Big Cypress National Preserve (right). Once plentiful, the animals are now extremely rare. Only 50 or so survive in the entire Everglades region.

AT A GLANCE . . .

If you like wildlife, you will like Everglades National Park. The park (as well as the adjoining Big Cypress National Preserve) is open all year. It's one of the best places in the Americas for observing wildlife up close in its natural habitat.

Old hands say the winter (dry) season is by far the best time to visit. That's when animals concentrate around gator holes and ponds. Another advantage of winter: Mosquitoes, sand flies, and other biting insects are less numerous. In summer, they can be unbearable. The insects never take a vacation, however, so take along insect repellent whatever the season. Shorts are not recommended.

The Everglades is not a bold land of towering peaks and rushing streams. Rather, it's a quiet, delicate wetland. Read about it in advance. Learn what to look for. Then, take your time as you go on your park adventure.

The park has four visitor centers. Although three do not offer lodging or meals, these facilities are available in nearby cities. The fourth center, Flamingo, lies 38 miles into the park on Florida Bay. It has extensive facilities, including food and lodging. Flamingo is the turnaround point in a visit to the Glades.

For more information write—
Superintendent, Everglades National Park, Box 279, Homestead, FL 33030

(Continued from page 28) stay in the park. "The water is clean, and the air smells good," says Samuel, 14. "It's so much quieter and more peaceful than in the city. You get to see nature up close. It's a real adventure."

33 "Everybody's favorites." That's how park ranger Karen Minkowski describes the Anhinga and Gumbo Limbo Trails. They lie just a few miles inside the park's southeastern entrance. The trails are short, less than half a mile each. But they give visitors with limited time an overall view of the park—and an understanding of its importance.

"I saw many things I never saw before," says Loubens Jean-Louis, 12. "I saw alligators. I also saw flocks of wading birds. And there were fish, turtles, and snakes. I wasn't afraid of the alligators and snakes. They keep their distance." Loubens says hiking the trails and observing the surroundings made him realize how important it is to protect the Glades. "There has to be a natural place for people to go to see animals," he says, "not just the zoo."

A hiker, if very lucky, might spot a Florida panther. "It's the rarest animal in the park," says ranger Minkowski. "There may be a dozen of them here in the park and 35 more in the surrounding parts of the Everglades. And that's it." The cats once ranged across the entire Southeast.

The American bald eagle, endangered in some places, finds a home in the park. So do many other rare or endangered animals. Among them are the American crocodile, the manatee or sea cow, the sandhill crane, and the peregrine falcon.

These animals all depend largely on the Everglades for their survival. And the Everglades depends on wise water management for *its* survival. Says Loubens Jean-Louis: "The park needs our help. We want all the animals to live. All my friends decided the same thing."

3 | Learning the Ropes In YOSEMITE

Secured by a strong line, climber Louis Poimiroo, 10, scales a steep rock face. Louis is learning rock climbing on Puppy Dome, a formation in California's Yosemite National Park. Once at the top, he'll have a breathtaking view of Yosemite's peaks and valleys.

> **'When we try to pick out anything by itself, we find it hitched to everything else in the universe.'**
>
> —John Muir,
> father of Yosemite National Park

In the 1860s, an adventurer and scientist named John Muir hiked alone in a remote wilderness high in California's Sierra Nevada. What Muir found filled him with awe. The sights surrounding him seemed as if they could easily overwhelm a giant, to say nothing of an ordinary man.

Sheer walls of granite rose thousands of feet above a green, forested valley. Rounded domes of polished rock gleamed in the sun. Waterfalls spilled gracefully over high cliffs and thundered as they reached the ground below. Mighty trees a hundred feet around stood guard in quiet forests.

In a journal he faithfully kept, Muir wrote that he had discovered a "glorious wilderness." The wilderness was Yosemite. As a result of Muir's

In history's footsteps

Dressed as 19th-century naturalist John Muir, actor Lee Stetson spins yarns for Yosemite visitors (below). Muir spent years exploring the region and recording its features. He helped persuade Congress to preserve Yosemite as a national park.

GALEN ROWELL

The power of ice   *Long ago, glaciers sculpted and refined*

much of Yosemite. Glacial action caused the cutoff shape that gives Half Dome, at upper right, its name.

Fallen giant

Schoolchildren from Carmichael, California, take a break on the roots of a giant sequoia (left). With bark two feet thick and branches bigger around than full-grown oak trees, sequoias are the largest living things on earth. Some at Yosemite have been growing for nearly 3,000 years. Right: A visitor peeks out from a cavernous hollow in a fallen sequoia.

GALEN ROWELL

YOSEMITE NATIONAL PARK

efforts, it became a national park. Today, visitors feel the same sense of wonder that Muir described.

"When you first see Yosemite, you wonder how a place like that could have been formed," says Louis Poimiroo, who lives in the park. Indians told of its beginnings in legends. They spoke of living rock that grew until it reached the sky. Miners who journeyed to California in search of gold described giant boulders sliced like loaves of bread, and trees big enough to drive a stagecoach through. Early American artists painted pictures of Yosemite—but people who saw the paintings didn't believe such a place existed.

Muir spent years hiking the Yosemite wilderness, searching for clues to its beginnings. He found scratches on rocks, and boulders that had been moved as if by a giant hand. Such signs convinced Muir that long ago the land had indeed been visited by giants—in this case, giant masses of snow and ice formed into glaciers.

Muir, it seems, was right. Between two and three million years ago, scientists say, much of North America lay under ice. During this period, snow fell continually on the Sierra Nevada year after year. Masses of unmelted snow hardened into glaciers, some half a mile thick. They moved through Yosemite Valley, gouging it deeper and wider. The glaciers did much of the sculpting of Yosemite's sheer cliffs, jagged peaks, and rounded domes.

Romp in a golden meadow

Hunting for insects, a young visitor—and junior ranger—sweeps a net over tall grasses. With the help of an adult ranger, she'll identify her catch and release it unharmed. The junior ranger program teaches youngsters about responsible park use.

39

'The most beautiful place on earth.'

—President Theodore Roosevelt
on Yosemite National Park

A stream fed by snowy peaks

Kendra Rudolph, 8, drops her line into the Merced River. Her fishing pole outlines El Capitan— "The Chief"—world's largest bare stone cliff. Downstream from Kendra, Travis Keay, 12, tries his luck. Both youngsters live in the park.

Rock slide

Youngsters try out a slide made by nature (right). Glaciers shaped and polished many of Yosemite's rock-dome formations. Others, like this one, formed when outer layers of rock split, then peeled away like layers of onion, leaving smooth mounds behind.

GALEN ROWELL

Curious to see one of nature's wonderworks, early visitors took long, winding journeys on horseback to reach the remote valley. Today's explorers follow in their footsteps—arriving by automobile or by bus. Sometimes they saddle up burros for a day's ride along old Yosemite trails.

"We rode where Indians once hunted and fished," says Ben Perry, 9, of El Portal, California. "It was dusty and bumpy. After a morning's ride, we were ready for a rest."

Ben's group tied up on a bank of the Merced River for a picnic. The youngsters played old Indian games and listened to the guides' stories about Yosemite—such as the one about the visit of the king of Belgium. As the story goes, all was quite formal and proper until one morning at breakfast. Then—"Hey, king!" shouted the cook across the campfire, "shoot me that side of bacon, will

41

ABCs of rock climbing

At the base of Puppy Dome, instructor Ellie Hawkins checks climbers' harnesses and safety ropes (above). The climbers are, from the left, Travis and his sister Tracy, 11; Louis and his sister Nicole, 12; and Brian Reilly, 12, all of Yosemite. Before climbing begins, youngsters learn the proper use of special rock-climbing equipment and garb, such as that shown at right. It includes—

A. gear sling (helps carry equipment), **B.** rescue pulley, **C.** headband or hat, **D.** rope, **E.** wedges (slip into cracks in rock), **F.** hexagonal chock (like wedge, but used for wider cracks), **G.** helmet (worn where there are loose rocks), **H.** work gloves, **I.** harness, **J.** locking carabiners (car-uh-BEE-nerz—rope is threaded through them), **K.** figure-eight device (for rappelling, or descending a slope), **L.** camming device (like chock, but used for even wider cracks), **M.** multi-purpose nylon webbing, **N.** nonlocking carabiners, **O.** sweatshirt, **P.** climbing shoes, **Q.** chalk bag (for drying hands), **R.** water bottle, **S.** backpack, **T.** lip balm, **U.** sunscreen, **V.** binoculars, **W.** sunglasses, **X.** loose-fitting pants, **Y.** T-shirt, **Z.** trained rock climber.

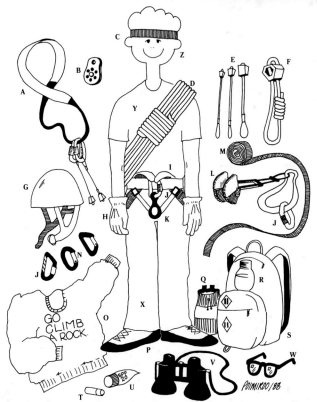

Not a small matter

With Hawkins's help, Nicole practices tying a knot called a figure eight. "The knots aren't difficult," says Nicole, "but it takes practice to do them right." A climber's life rests on properly tied knots.

Going down!

Grinning with confidence, Nicole gets set to rappel a slope. "Rappelling was great," she said after the descent. "It felt so good to know I could do it!"

you?" Stunned silence: Royalty addressed in such a tone? But, with a laugh, the king tossed over the bacon. The cook and the king became fast friends.

Aside from being an ideal place for swimming and storytelling, the Merced provides sport for fishermen—but there's something of a catch. "The fish are choosy," says Brian Reilly, 12, of Yosemite. "It's best to use natural bait like worms and bugs. You also have to be very patient."

Several trails lead into forests of giant sequoias, the park's oldest inhabitants. "The trees are bigger than you can imagine," says Amanda Harris, 12, of El Portal. "It took 30 people joining hands to circle just one of them." Some of the red-barked giants, scientists say, sprouted almost 3,000 years ago. They're still growing.

Along the trails, the adventurers looked skyward at towering cliffs and peaks. At the valley's lower end, they passed El Capitan—"The Chief." It is the largest exposed block of granite in the world. Nearby, the Three Brothers, named for the sons of an Indian chief, form a rocky peak three quarters of a mile high.

Nearing the cliffs, the visitors saw—and heard—some of the highest waterfalls in the world. At Yosemite Falls, the water plunges nearly half a mile in three stages. The final drop alone is twice the height of Niagara Falls. "The falls make a giant rumbling sound," says Brian. "It's like thunder."

Yosemite's boulders, domes, and cliffs present adventurers with a new challenge—rock climbing. "Yosemite is the best place in the world to rock climb," says Amanda. "I thought it would be hard, but almost anyone can do it with the right instructor and proper equipment."

The Yosemite Mountaineering School provides both instruction and equipment. The school is privately run but falls under the general supervision of the National Park Service. It offers classes to new climbers young and old.

Classes begin on the lower slope of a formation known as Pothole Dome. It's a fairly easy rise, with a lot of cracks for getting a grip. The basics—safety and equipment—are covered first. "Climbers

Between a rock and a hard place

Above the treetops, Louis rappels Puppy Dome's hundred-foot overhang (right). By easing the rope through his hands, Louis controls his speed. Other climbers watch from below.

AT A GLANCE . . .

Yosemite is considered one of the world's most scenic parks. For all its natural beauty, however, Yosemite lies surprisingly close to large urban centers. It is only a four-hour drive from the San Francisco Bay area, and even less from cities such as Sacramento and Fresno. Because of the relative ease, for many, of driving to Yosemite, overcrowding is becoming a problem in some areas. Rangers advise visitors to make early reservations for campgrounds and other overnight facilities — especially for weekend and holiday stays.

It is still possible, though, to get away from it all. Yosemite's 750 miles of trails fan out over a vast region of backcountry. Roughing it, a team of campers or hikers could go for weeks without seeing any other human beings (although visitors are limited to a seven-day stay).

The park offers three major features: alpine wilderness, groves of giant sequoias, and Yosemite Valley. From one region to another, the climate can change dramatically. At the same time summer snow flurries are dusting a mountain peak, the valley may be experiencing a heat wave. Packing clothes for a variety of weather conditions will help you make the most of a trip to Yosemite. *For more information write—* Superintendent, Yosemite National Park, Box 577, Yosemite, CA   95389.

wear special shoes with soles that won't easily slip or skid," says Travis Keay, 12, of Yosemite. "You use climber's rope and learn to tie knots correctly. The knots help keep you safe, so you practice until you can tie them exactly right every time."

Travis's group first learned to "free climb." In free climbing, a minimum of equipment is used. Finding secure handholds and footholds, the climbers slowly went up the dome's face. Each wore a safety rope attached to a harness around the waist. An instructor watched from above. If a climber were to slip, the instructor would hold the safety line tight, preventing a fall.

The next day, the climbers used their newly found skills to go up a formation called Puppy Dome. "I kept thinking about the summit, 80 feet up," says Nicole Poimiroo, 12, Louis's sister. "I knew I would make it."

For many climbers, the best was yet to come. The way down is over a steep cliff on the opposite side of the dome. Using a technique called rappelling (ruh-PEL-ing), the youngsters lowered themselves down the sheer wall. Lines anchored at the top of the cliff supported their weight and enabled them to control the speed of descent. The instructor held the safety lines from above. "Rappelling is a little scary at first," says Brian. "Then you start to really enjoy it." "It's great," agrees Amanda. "It feels like flying free!"

In his journal, John Muir wrote about the wilderness he loved: "Every rock seems to glow with life. No temple made with human hands can compare with Yosemite." Muir urged that visitors "climb the mountains and get their good tidings."

And so they do. Whether climbing the park's granite peaks or hiking its wilderness trails, explorers of Yosemite share a common feeling. Travis, the young mountain climber, is no exception. "There's no place like Yosemite," he says. "You want to come back and do it all again."

44

4 | Biking Along CAPE COD

Beside grassy sand dunes, two bikers pedal across land the Pilgrims explored. Here at Cape Cod National Seashore, visitors plunge into history and into the area's long seafaring tradition. The cape offers vacationers a variety of activities the year round.

'All around are sand dunes—
huge piles of sand with grass
holding it together.'

—Michael Riordan, 10

The land that forms Cape Cod juts into the sea from Massachusetts like a giant arm bent at the elbow. At its northern end the land curves inward—a hand beckoning visitors to its shores. From elbow to fingers, the land stretches for 40 miles. Much of this land forms Cape Cod National Seashore.

On the seashore's winding bicycle trails, visitors pedal along stretches of sand backed by towering dunes. Ponds and grassy marshes dot the landscape. Cool, shadowy forests contrast with warm, sunny beaches. Danny Kline, 10, and a group of other youngsters explored the seashore in the summertime by bicycle. "Bicycling is a good way to get to know the cape," says Danny. Along the way, Danny and the other youngsters also learned about the cape's seafaring history.

"Many sights on Cape Cod, such as the lighthouses along the shore, remind you of life here long ago," says Danny, whose home is in Brewster, Massachusetts. "Before lighthouses were built, ships had an especially rough time navigating around the cape." Even today the cape can be treacherous. In the winter months, violent storms lash the area. Howling winds rake the ocean, building mountainous waves that sometimes dash seagoing craft onto sandbars.

It was by sea that the cape's earliest visitors arrived. Seventeenth-century explorers described a land rich in animals, trees, and fish. One of the explorers named the cape for the great numbers of codfish he found swimming in its bay.

"One ship that nearly was lost off Cape Cod was the *Mayflower,*" says Danny. "It was headed

Signpost of the sea

Race Point Light shines out to ships at sea from Cape Cod's northern tip. For nearly 200 years, lighthouses on the cape have warned navigators of waters made treacherous by storms and shoals. Still, the cape has seen its share of shipwrecks— more than 3,000 in the past 300 years.

south of the cape, toward the Hudson River, but then it ran into trouble." The water became shallow, and waves started to drive the ship toward shore. The captain decided to turn north.

At the northern end of the cape, the captain felt his way into the deep, protected waters of what is now Provincetown Harbor. With the ship safely at anchor, Captain Miles Standish and the ship's captain and crew explored the cape. To the west, across Cape Cod Bay, they found a good area for settlement. *Mayflower* weighed anchor on December 15, 1620. The ship sailed for the place that would soon be named Plymouth. It would become the first successful English colony in New England.

Early settlers on the cape found thick forests of oak, pine, beech, and cedar. Settlers cut down many of the trees to build houses and ships. They cleared land to plant crops and to graze cattle. By the late 1700s, most of the forests were gone from Cape Cod.

Without trees or other vegetation to hold the earth down, the topsoil blew away. Winds piled up sand in high dunes. Thus the landscape visitors see today is different from that of a few hundred years ago. "Riding along in some places, all you see is dunes," says Michael Riordan, 10, of Eastham, Massachusetts. "There are only a few pine trees near the shore. They're stunted from the strong winds."

To hold back the blowing sand, cape residents in the early 1800s planted hundreds of acres of beach grass. It has long roots that hold the sand in place. Such conservation efforts have helped the

New paths, old land

Bicyclists ride along Province Lands Trail, one of several at the seashore (opposite). Along the way, they saw a spattering of red at trailside and decided to stop. It was a cranberry bog (below).

'Red gold'

That's what early growers called the bright red fruit (above). Settlers cooked wild cranberries into breads, jams, and sauces after Indians showed them that the tart fruit could be eaten.

Cranberry sampling ground

In the bog, youngsters test the pucker power of the sour fruit (above). Cranberries both wild and cultivated thrive in the wet, sandy soil of Cape Cod's marshes. The cape itself was formed as glaciers pushed rock, gravel, and sand into place some 20,000 years ago. Then the glaciers retreated. Wind and sea have been shaping the land ever since.

CAPE COD NATIONAL SEASHORE

land recover. Within the national seashore, trees and wildflowers are making a comeback on land that was bare a hundred years ago.

Wheeling along a low-lying area, the bikers spotted a splash of red near the trail. The Pilgrims were greeted by the same sight—cranberries. Indians taught the settlers how to prepare the sour fruit so it was fit to eat. Settlers then began harvesting berries they found growing in bogs, or swamps. The berries are rich in vitamin C. Sailors on long voyages found that eating them could prevent scurvy, a then common shipboard disease.

Cranberries—"red gold," they were called—provided a livelihood for colonists. Growers still harvest cranberries commercially at bogs inside the national seashore. On invitation, the bikers stopped at such a bog to taste its treasure. They didn't eat much. "Raw cranberries are *really* sour," says Danny. "They made my mouth pucker!"

The biking trail leads to Race Point Beach, at the northern point of the cape. Here the winter winds howl and fling stinging sheets of sand. Here, and on beaches to the south, more than 3,000 ships have met with disaster.

At Race Point stood the first in a string of nine lifesaving stations built in the late 1800s. They belonged to an organization called the U. S. Life-Saving Service. For the ten stormiest months of the year, the service patrolled the beach day and night. Even in the blackest and foulest of weather, at the

Up, up, and away!

Strong winds carry a kite aloft on Province Lands Beach (above). With the help of his father, Steve, 12-year-old Keith Loughane controls the strings. "On the beach," says Keith, "the breezes are great for kite flying." Keith's hometown, nearby Provincetown, Massachusetts, was the site of the Pilgrims' landing in the New World, in 1620.

cry of "Ship ashore!" a seven-man team would board a surfboat and row over mountainous seas to rescue survivors. The lifesavers' unofficial motto: "You have to go, but you don't have to come back."

The Life-Saving Service would later become part of the United States Coast Guard. The official motto of the service remains as the Coast Guard's motto: *Semper Paratus*—Always Ready.

Nature is constantly at work on Cape Cod. The great arm of the cape is the work of glaciers that moved across parts of North America some 20,000 years ago. The glaciers carried sand, gravel, and rock with them as they inched their way southward. As the climate warmed, the glaciers melted. They left behind the rocky deposits that form the Cape Cod peninsula.

"All around you, you see how the wind, the rain, and especially the ocean shape the land," says Catriona Rayl, of Marlboro, Vermont. Catriona, 14, and a group of classmates took part in an environmental education program sponsored by the National Park Service. For a week, the youngsters lived in the Eastham Coast Guard Station, at Nauset Beach, on lower Cape Cod.

"The ocean was our front door, and Nauset Marsh our back," says Jason MacArthur, 13. "On the beach and marsh trails, we had a chance to see the cape's different environments."

The trails start at Salt Pond, one of the cape's so-called kettle ponds. Kettle ponds formed when blocks of glacial ice melted, leaving kettles—craterlike depressions—in the ground. Dozens of these kettles, filled with fresh or salt water, dot the cape.

A narrow channel connects Salt Pond to Nauset Marsh. When early explorers charted Cape Cod, Nauset Marsh was a harbor deep enough for sailing ships. But sand and silt carried in by the ocean slowly filled the harbor, forming swampy land. Over time, the salt marsh developed there.

"A barrier beach protects the marsh from the force of the ocean," says Zachary Hulme, 14. "That

'Here a man may stand, and put all
of America behind him.'

—Naturalist Henry David Thoreau
at Race Point Beach, 1846

Bareback at the beach

*Rosemary Henrique, in front, and Michelle Martin
ride horses on a beachside trail. "The beaches are
a peaceful place to ride or just walk," says
Rosemary. "You can really relax here." The girls,
both 15, live in Provincetown.*

'. . . By the beautiful sea . . . .' *At the Eastham Coast Guard Station overlooking the Atlantic Ocean, students fro*

...Marlboro, Vermont, start up a game of stickball.

Cape Cod's history reaches back a long way, yet the seashore is one of the most recent additions to the national park system. It was established in 1966. The seashore gets most of its visitors during summer. Visiting the park in winter, many say, is the best way to witness the land-shaping powers of wind and sea.

During summer, five beaches are open to the public. Swimming outside the public beaches is prohibited. There are no lifeguards in undesignated areas.

A web of roads allows motorists to reach just about every part of the seashore with ease. There are also hiking and bicycle trails in the most scenic areas. Bicycles can be rented in Provincetown and Orleans. Horses, also available for rent, are restricted to certain trails.

Fishing and shellfishing are popular activities. You may need a license. No camping is allowed at the seashore, but private campgrounds are available nearby.

For more information write— Superintendent, Cape Cod National Seashore, South Wellfleet, MA 02663

makes the marsh a good breeding ground for fish and birds. We saw hundreds of clam shells dropped by feeding birds. We also saw big round shells shed by horsehoe crabs."

North of Nauset Marsh, visitors get an idea of the ocean's power to shape the land. In 1901, the Italian physicist Guglielmo Marconi built four tall wooden towers on the sandy cliffs there. Marconi sent the first telegraphic message across the Atlantic Ocean from the towers. Today the land where they once stood is gone, claimed by the sea.

Year after year, the ocean continues to pound the cape's sandy shores, reshaping the coastline. "What someone finds here today is different from what visitors will see in years to come," says Catriona. "Cape Cod is a place of constant change."

5 | PACIFIC RIM
Three Parks In One

Pleased to meet you! At an island in Pacific Rim National Park, a young kayaker pauses to watch a group of sea lions. Pacific Rim lies on Canada's rugged west coast, in the province of British Columbia. In addition to sea islands, the park has beaches and forested wilderness. It offers a range of activities to match.

'It was paddle as fast as we could— or crash against the rocks. . . . '

—Chelsea Rae, 15

The kayakers paddled quietly into the bay. Ahead, about 200 California sea lions rested on the rocks. Chelsea Rae, 15, of Campbell River, British Columbia, pulled in for a closer look. Suddenly, with barks that rang in Chelsea's ears, the sea lions began slipping into the water. They headed for another island, but Chelsea was in the way.

"Some of them were hitting their heads on the bottom of the kayak," she says. "It was tipping back and forth. That was really scary."

But Chelsea's kayak didn't turn over. "I don't think they noticed they were hitting me," she says. "They were just in a hurry."

A close encounter with sea lions is just one of many adventures possible in Pacific Rim National Park, on Canada's west coast. It has everything from sandy beaches to rugged islands to thickly forested trails. The changing landscape holds a wide variety of plants and animals.

Pacific Rim hugs the southwest coast of Vancouver Island, in British Columbia. The park consists of three separate sections. Northernmost is Long Beach, a strip of seashore 16 miles long. In the middle lie the Broken Group Islands, nearly a hundred islands and islets in Barkley Sound. The West Coast Trail makes up the southernmost section of the park. Hikers can trek nearly 50 miles along the rugged trail.

Chelsea and five friends, all from British Columbia (as are most of the other adventurers in this chapter), visited the Broken Group Islands during the summer. For some of the youngsters, such as Jeremy Petch, 11, it was the first time ever

Treacherous passage

Timing counts in paddling through a formation called the Tunnel. Waves roll into it from both ends, crashing in the middle. "The trick is to pass through quickly between waves," says Josie Boulding, in the lead. Close behind Josie are Chelsea Rae and Elisa Jackovich. The youngsters, all 15, live in Campbell River, in British Columbia—home province also of most of the other adventurers in this chapter.

Lengthy subject

Josie examines a string of giant kelp. Beds of the plant, rooted in the seafloor, may stretch for miles. They create a habitat rich in marine life.

Taking a break

Elisa, left, and Chelsea pause to catch their breath. "Kayaking becomes quite tiring after a while, and your back gets sore," says Chelsea. Elisa adds, "The trip meant a lot of work and time, but it was worth every moment!" The kayakers paddled among the Broken Group Islands, one of the three separate areas that make up the park.

to go kayaking in the ocean. Jeremy, who lives in Victoria, says simply, "I was quite scared."

And not without reason. At Effingham Island, largest in the Broken Group, the sea has bored a tunnel through the rock (page 58). Seawater swells into both ends and waves crash in the middle.

"The waves make a big explosion, and all the water rushes through very fast," Jeremy says. Adds Chelsea, "Sometimes there were really vicious waves. We thought we would smash against the wall."

Only about 30 seconds of calm separates each collision of the waves. To get through, a kayaker must wait at one end of the 30-foot tunnel until the waves crash, then paddle quickly to the other end before the waves surge toward each other again. With careful timing, everyone made it through safely.

By conquering the tunnel, Jeremy proved something to himself. "I learned a lot more about how well I could kayak," he says. "I never really knew I could do that. That was a big step."

During the spring, visitors to Long Beach watch for gray whales offshore. The whales, some of which grow longer than a touring bus, pass Pacific Rim each spring on their way to summer feeding grounds farther north. Along the beach, the park has set up a number of viewing stations equipped with telescopes.

The best view, however, is from a boat. Stacey Nimmo, 14, of Ucluelet, got so close to the whales in a boat that she could touch them. "They were coming under the boat, and they would come up and let you pet them," she says. "They're so playful. They chase each other around and then come back near the boat." Back on land, Stacey got a close look at a bald eagle. She was walking on Long Beach when the eagle landed on a log ten feet away. She held very still, watching the bird. "After a while," she says, "it just flew away."

"Long Beach is really a nice place," says Krista Brown, 14, of Nanaimo. "It doesn't have lots of seaweed to get tangled up in as you wade. The beach is sandy, and the waves are big." During the summer,

Time of the whale

Its head just breaking the water, a Pacific gray whale glides along the Canadian coast (right). Every spring the entire population of Pacific grays—some 19,000 whales—passes by Pacific Rim. They're headed for arctic waters on their annual migration from mating grounds off Mexico. At the peak of the season, park visitors may see dozens of whales in only a few hours.

JEFF FOOTT

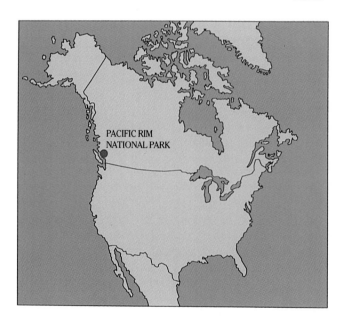

PACIFIC RIM
NATIONAL PARK

60

Long haul

James Brown, 16, of Nanaimo, drags a rope of giant kelp across Long Beach, the second section of the park. Commercial firms harvest the plant. It yields vitamins, minerals, and a substance used as a smoothing agent in such foods as ice cream.

the waves may rise ten feet high. In winter, storms whip up the ocean, sending breakers as tall as three-story houses crashing against the beach. Salt spray splashes a hundred feet into the air.

Krista's brother James spotted an uprooted strip of giant kelp floating in the water. He dragged it ashore to show his family. "I didn't realize how long it was at first," he says. "It turned out to be 15 feet long." Actually, the plant was on the short side. Rooted to the seafloor, stalks of giant kelp often grow to more than 200 feet.

James tested the waters. "Near shore, the water is warm enough for swimming," he reports, "but it's too cold for me farther out." That was in summer, when the inshore water temperature was about 59°F—crisp enough. In winter, the temperature slides to a chilly 45°F or so. Some daredevils swim and surf year-round, but most are content just to walk on the beach, getting their toes wet.

When the tide goes out at Long Beach, people gather at rocky places in the intertidal zone. That's the strip of shore between the high-water mark and the low-water mark. The zone teems with sea life. In fact, the intertidal life at Pacific Rim may be the richest in the world. Mussels and barnacles cling to the black rocks. Urchins, sea stars, sponges, and sea anemones fill the tidal pools, along with tiny fish and crabs.

"This was the first time I'd really seen a sea star," says Melanie Parkin, 15, of Revelstoke, Alberta. "I didn't know where to look for them before." Melanie and her family spent several nights camping at the park. Early one morning they walked along the intertidal zone with park interpreter Marla Oliver.

"One reason the intertidal zone is so rich with sea life is the temperate climate," Oliver says. "It never gets either very hot or very cold here. Another reason is a condition called upwelling." Upwelling occurs as strong currents sweep the ocean bottom. The currents stir up nutrients that feed plankton— the tiny plants and animals upon which many fish

63

©TIM FITZHARRIS

Romp on the beach

A low wave splashes James's sisters, Karla, 12, at left, and Krista, 14, as they wade ankle deep in the surf. The girls enjoy chasing tiny fish and playing on the beach. "The sand is nice and hard," says Krista. "It's perfect for building sand castles."

Preening pipers

While waiting for the tide to uncover their feeding ground, western sandpipers clean their feathers. The birds are a common sight along the shore.

feed. The more plankton, the more fish and other creatures that come to eat.

Oliver encourages visitors to touch the strange-looking sea life. "People are sometimes afraid to put their hands in the water," she says, "but the only things that could harm you here are jellyfish—and their sting doesn't last."

The winds that sweep into Pacific Rim carry a heavy burden of moisture from the ocean. They drop that burden along the coast. Over many thousands of years, the drizzle and the frequent

downpours have helped produce a lush rain forest.

Some trees in the park have been alive for a thousand years. And some are among the largest in the world. Sitka spruce tower over the beach like 25-story buildings. Unlike most trees, Sitka spruce thrive on salt spray, and they act as windbreaks for other, less hardy trees. Another variety, the Western red cedar, has a trunk so big around that it would take 14 people with outstretched arms to encircle one that is fully grown.

Nowhere is the forest more lush than along the West Coast Trail—the third section of the park. "The undergrowth *(Continued on page 69)*

A heron's eagle eye

Its head cocked for a better view, a great blue heron peers at stalks of bull kelp. The kelp attracts large numbers of fish and other sea life. Once it spots prey, the heron will nab it in its spearlike bill. Pacific Rim shelters a large variety of wildlife.

©TIM FITZHARRIS

Star of the show

Park interpreters help give visitors an appreciation of wildlife. Here, Marla Oliver shows a purple sea star to a group that includes Melanie and her twin brothers, Robert and Ben. Among the creatures found in the intertidal zone, sea stars are especially common. "Sea creatures are very different from us," Oliver says, "but their function, like ours, is the same. It is survival: finding food, finding a mate, finding shelter."

'Ouch! Hey, watch it! Ow!'

A close-up of red sea urchins shows the spines that serve as a defense and help them move. The spines are also used in feeding. Sea urchins eat mainly seaweed, but just about anything will do.

Life in the intertidal zone

Like most other beaches, Long Beach has two high tides and two low tides every day. The area between the low-water mark and the high-water mark makes up the intertidal zone. It supports an abundance of sea life. Some creatures are trapped in pools as the tide retreats. Others swim among seaweed. Still others scurry on the exposed beach, seeking food. Here, Melanie Parkin, 14, of Revelstoke, Alberta, and her brother Ben, 12, examine a red sea urchin found in a tidal pool.

Which is the purple sea star?

They all are—although only one has its namesake color. Despite their name, purple sea stars may be yellow, brown, reddish, or orange. A sea star takes an unusual approach to eating. It inserts its stomach *between the shell halves of its prey, such as a mussel. The stomach then digests the meat inside. "Instead of putting the food into its stomach, it puts its stomach into the food," says interpreter Oliver.*

AT A GLANCE . . .

Among national parks, Pacific Rim is a newcomer. It was established in 1970. The moderate climate allows visitors to enjoy the park year-round. The information center greets visitors daily from Easter to Thanksgiving.

Of the park's three sections, Long Beach is the most easily reached and the most visited. It offers swimming, fishing, camping, hiking, and public programs by park interpreters. Whale watching is at its best at Long Beach, especially between mid-March and mid-May.

To reach the Broken Group Islands, visitors must take a boat. Ferry service and rental boats are available. The islands vary from tiny rocks to landforms big enough for hiking and camping.

For true roughing it, visitors seek out the West Coast Trail. It can be reached by car. The trail is long. Park officials strongly recommend that only experienced hikers and campers attempt to cover the entire route.

Ocean swimming may be cold for those not used to it. Currents and tidal flows can be strong. Be certain to follow safety rules for ocean swimming and wading. If you go rock-hopping in the intertidal zone, check whether the tide is rising or falling. You don't want to be stranded on an island when the tide is coming in.

For more information write—
Superintendent, Pacific Rim National Park, Box 280, Ucluelet, British Columbia, Canada V0R 3A0

'How many toothpicks . . . ?'

Peter Stevens, 11, on the left, and Aaron Mundy, 11, both of Ucluelet, crane their necks at a 300-foot-tall Sitka spruce (left). The spruce is a common sight along the West Coast Trail, the park's third section. The trail challenges the most experienced hikers.

Beautiful bandit

A Steller's jay, official bird of British Columbia, perches on a tree limb. The jays are brightly colored— and pesky. They often snatch food from campsites.

THOMAS KITCHIN/FIRST LIGHT

(Continued from page 64)   makes for hard hiking," says Aaron Mundy, 11, of Ucluelet. But Aaron loves the challenge. He enjoys the forest so much that he hopes to become a park interpreter.

Backpackers come to the trail in search of adventure. They have to know what they're doing. The trail stretches for 45 miles and takes at least 6 days to complete. At times, parts of the trail may disappear beneath the tide. Fallen trees are often the only bridges across rushing streams. The path is sometimes steep and slippery.

Other than hikers, the only people along the trail are Indians native to the region. Their tribal name, Nuu-chah-nulth, means "all along the mountains." Many of the Indians fish and cut trees for a living. A few maintain the trail and ferry backpackers across dangerous rivers.

In early days, the trail was used as a rescue route for survivors of shipwrecks. Now it's used for recreation. Hikers say its rugged beauty is unforgettable. "It's more varied and spectacular than other sections of the park," says interpreter Barry Campbell. "It's got it all: cliffs, strange sandstone formations, old lighthouses, and the remains of dozens of shipwrecks."

But no matter where visitors go in Pacific Rim, they are sure to have a wilderness adventure. As kayaker Chelsea Rae puts it: "The park is a rugged place. People almost seem out of place here. The park belongs to the ocean, the trees, and the animals."

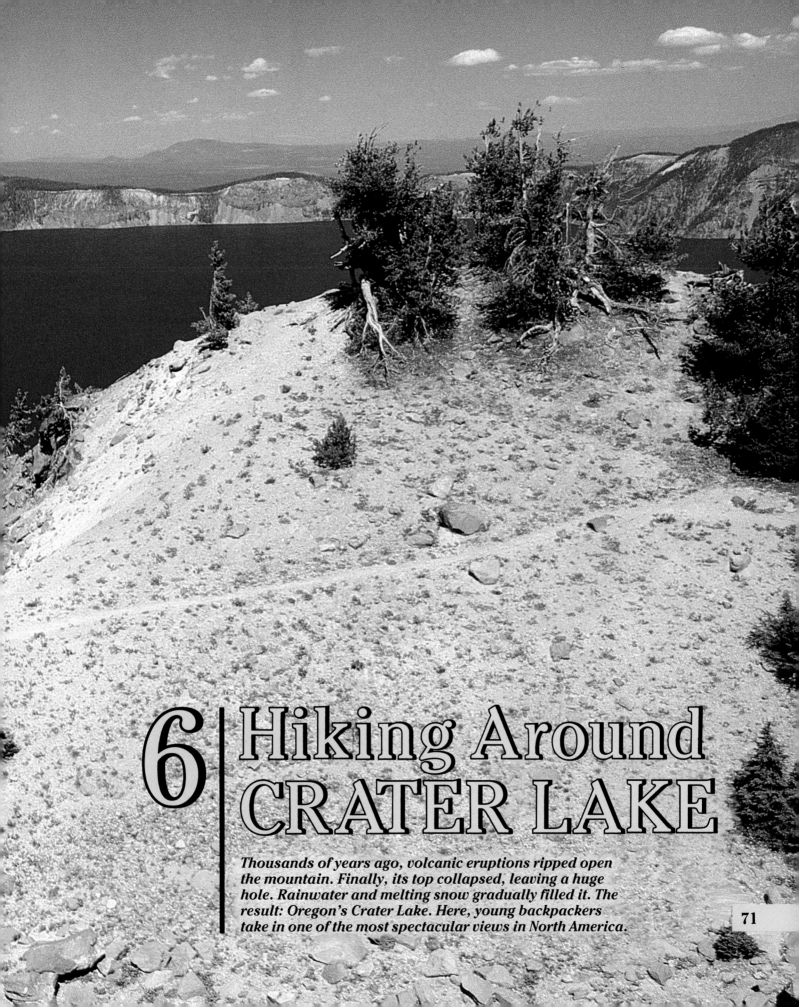

6 | Hiking Around CRATER LAKE

Thousands of years ago, volcanic eruptions ripped open the mountain. Finally, its top collapsed, leaving a huge hole. Rainwater and melting snow gradually filled it. The result: Oregon's Crater Lake. Here, young backpackers take in one of the most spectacular views in North America.

71

'I loved the clean mountain air, the smell of the fresh pines. . . .'

—Dean Nakanishi, 12

℘ "Crater Lake has magnificent blues and greens," says Amber Kopel, 13, of Santa Cruz, California. "I liked the way you could look over the entire lake from up above and see all the trees in the park."

"The water was so clear and so blue," says Andre Miller, 13, of San Mateo, California, "I'd never seen anything like it!"

Amber and Andre were describing an adventure they had in Crater Lake National Park with seven other California youngsters. Led by wilderness guide Craig Richardson, the group hiked over rugged terrain around the lake's rim. Their journey carried them to the top of a mountain, through forests, and across fields of volcanic rock. They wound up the trip by crossing the lake and exploring an island created by the same volcanic activity that formed Crater Lake itself.

For hundreds of thousands of years, a volcano, Mount Mazama, towered where Crater Lake now lies. Then, about 6,800 years ago, after repeated eruptions, the top of the volcano collapsed. The caldera, or huge crater, that was left measured 6 miles across. It gradually filled with snowmelt and rainwater, and the lake was born. At 1,932 feet, it is the deepest lake in the United States.

Klamath Indians lived in the area and saw the awesome eruptions. Through the centuries, the Indians came to consider Crater Lake as sacred. They believed it was the home of a powerful spirit. Tradition prohibited them from visiting the lake, or even gazing upon it.

In 1853, prospectors came. They asked the Klamath about the lake. Perhaps not wishing to

Cold morning, hot meal

Bundled up against the early chill, Dean Nakanishi, 12, of San Mateo, scrambles breakfast eggs over a crackling fire. "We all helped prepare meals," says Dean. "We worked well as a team." The hikers burned and then buried leftover food, leaving each campsite clean for the next visitors.

Foiling animal prowlers

Andre Miller, 13, of San Mateo, California, hangs bags holding food and gear on a line stretched between two trees. That keeps the supplies out of reach of rodents and other nighttime visitors.

Reward at day's end

Enjoying the warm glow, the backpackers, all from California, relax around a campfire. Every night, the group played a game called spirit stick. Making a wish, each person shaved off a piece of the stick. On the last night, all the shavings were thrown into the fire in hope that the wishes would come true.

Easy does it

Though the trek took place in summer, winter snows lingered. Amber Kopel, of Santa Cruz (opposite), climbs on rocks alongside a 10-foot-high snowbank. "I tried to climb the snow," says Amber, 13, "but it was almost as hard as ice."

Blue sky, bluer water

Heads hidden by backpacks, three hikers pause for a view from the Garfield Peak Trail. In the background lies Wizard Island. At 8,060 feet, Garfield Peak is one of the highest points on the lake rim. "The height was scary at first," reports Josh Mallery, 11, of Aptos, "but I got used to it."

AT A GLANCE . . .

Crater Lake National Park welcomes visitors all year long. Meals, gifts, and film are sold daily at the Coffee Shop. Some facilities, such as the north entrance road, Rim Drive, and Crater Lake Lodge, are open only during summer. Check the situation before visiting the park.

Rim Drive, 33 miles around, gives an almost continuous view of the lake. Hikers may walk along Rim Drive or they can choose from a number of rugged trails.

Special regulations:

• Climbing inside the caldera to reach the lake is permitted only on the Cleetwood Trail.

• Private boats are not permitted on the lake.

• In the more heavily trafficked areas of the park, camping is permitted only at Mazama and Lost Creek Campgrounds. It is allowed in the backcountry by permit.

For more information write —
Superintendent, Crater Lake National Park, Box 7, Crater Lake, OR 97604

have the spirit disturbed, the Indians denied the lake's existence.

But the lake was now "discovered." Word of its exceptional beauty spread. So attractive is the lake that today it might be surrounded by condominiums and shopping malls—if it hadn't been for the newspaper wrapped around the lunch of one William Gladstone Steel. Steel was a Kansas schoolboy. The newspaper carried an article about Crater Lake. It caught Steel's eye and captured his interest. He resolved someday to see the lake.

Steel got his wish as an adult. He visited the lake in 1885. The natural beauty, still unspoiled, so overwhelmed him that he spent the next 17 years fighting to have the lake protected by law. His efforts paid off. In 1902, President Theodore Roosevelt declared the lake a national park. Today's visitors, such as the group led by guide Richardson, appreciate the same view that the prospectors found in 1853.

Rising early on their first day, the group hiked to the summit of 8,060-foot Garfield Peak. Many of the youngsters were not prepared for the steep heights they were to climb. "In one place the path was only about *(Continued on page 79)*

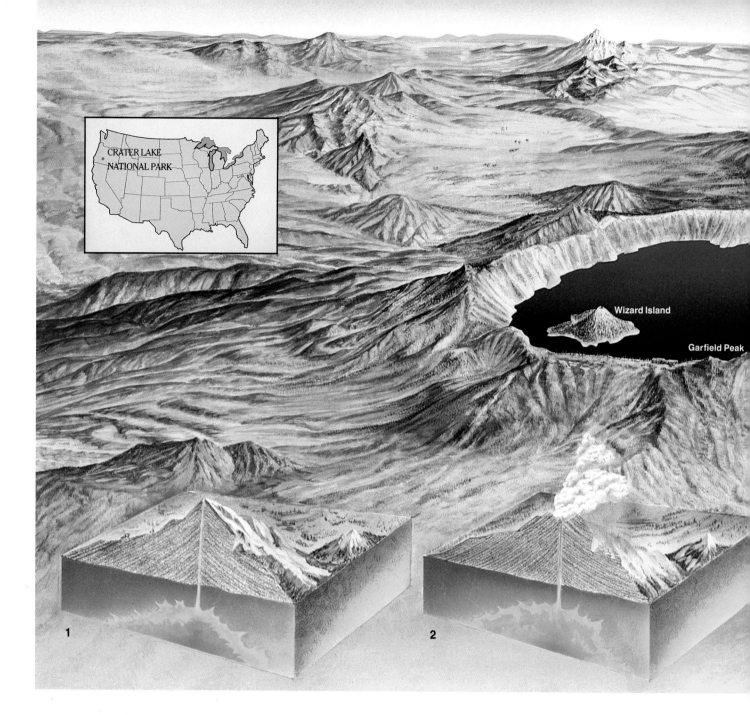

CRATER LAKE
NATIONAL PARK

Wizard Island

Garfield Peak

1

2

Battle of the mountain spirits

In a game called volcano, the hikers reenact the eruptions of Mount Mazama that caused the formation of Crater Lake (left). Indians in the region, the Klamath, actually saw the event some 6,800 years ago. In their legends, the earth's violence came in a battle between Llao, chief of the Below World, and Skell, chief of the Upper World. Llao lived in Mount Mazama; Skell lived in Mount Shasta a hundred miles to the south. The spirits fought with fire and smoke, lightning and thunder. Hot rocks dropped from the sky, and the sun disappeared for seven days. The legends say that two Klamath elders threw themselves into the volcano as a peace sacrifice. Grieving for their brave leaders, the people circled the volcano's rim. Their tears filled the caldera, or giant crater.

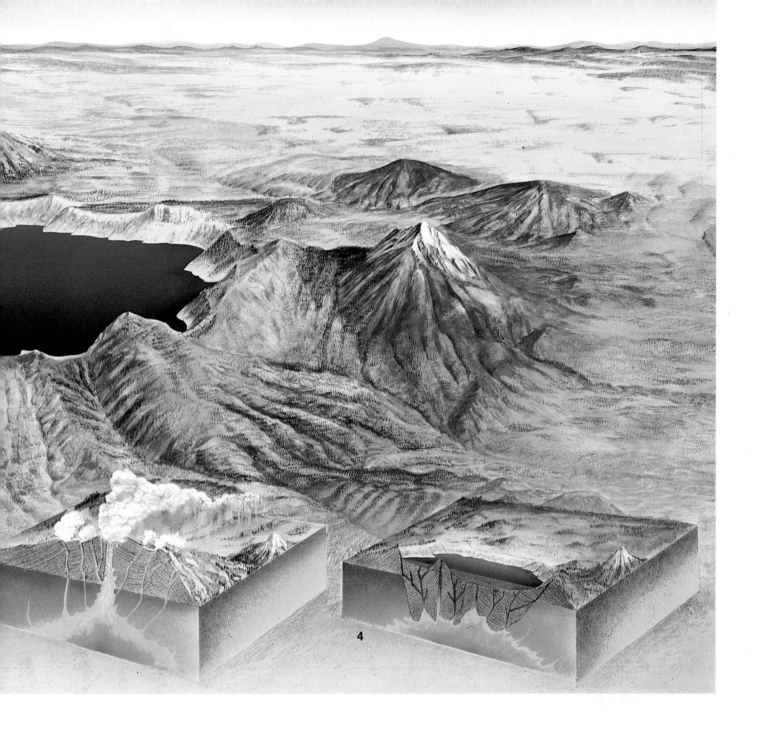

4

Geologists say that the Klamaths' description of fire and smoke and sunless days is accurate. The scientists, however, have their own explanation of how the lake formed (above). According to them, for millions of years along the coast of Oregon and Washington, one of the plates that make up the earth's crust has been sliding under another. At one point, magma—melted rock—pushed upward from the lower plate and reached the surface through a single vent. Over hundreds of thousands of years, there occurred a series of eruptions from that vent. *1)* The eruptions built Mount Mazama to a height of 12,000 feet. Other mountains in the Cascade Range formed in the same way. *2)* As the vent expanded, stored-up pressure from the main chamber was released, erupting at the surface. *3)* Lesser vents formed. About 4860 B.C. a series of huge eruptions blew out much of the cone. The mountain was left with no support, and collapsed. *4)* Over 600 to 800 years, rain and snow gradually filled the caldera. Today, the lake in the caldera is 1,932 feet deep.

Touch test

Using his fingertips, Vijaya Prisk, of Watsonville, examines the bark of a tree (right). Vijaya, 11, was led to the tree blindfolded and was told it was a mountain hemlock. Later, with his eyes uncovered, he could identify a hemlock by feeling the bark.

Ah, what a life!

On a break, Josh takes in the view from Wizard Island (left). The island volcano was the scene of Mount Mazama's last display of fireworks. "Crater Lake is beautiful up close," says Josh. "It's just like a picture."

(Continued from page 75) three and a half feet wide," recalls Dean Nakanishi, 12, of San Mateo. "Once I stumbled backward, next to the edge of the trail. It was terrifying! But when I reached the top, the spectacular view was worth it all."

Christine Meyer, 16, and Claire Shultz, 14, both of Santa Cruz, agree that the thrill of climbing Garfield Peak was the highlight of their trip. "I liked the way you could look down and see everything: the lake, the boats, and the island," says Claire.

During the five-day adventure, the group learned the value of teamwork. "The environment is unpredictable. It's important to cooperate, and make the best of what comes along," says Dean. "Cooperation helped us get through the tough times." The group shared cooking duties. They helped each other with their gear. When the going got rough, they gave each other encouragement.

On one stretch, the group discovered a snowbank about 30 feet wide and 10 feet high—a summer surprise. "We had a snow fight," says Josh Mallery, 11, of Aptos. "And buried in the snow I found a 1942 silver dime."

Another kind of surprise came one nightfall as the backpackers were making camp. "Suddenly the sky exploded with lightning and thunder," says Corrina Kopel, 9, of Santa Cruz. "I could see the trees as if it were daytime. I'd never been so close to lightning. It was very exciting!" The hikers had stopped for the night on low ground. That reduced their chances of being struck by lightning.

A trip by boat to Wizard Island, a volcano within Crater Lake, wound up the adventure. The trip gave the hikers a chance to see some of the lake's unusual features up close. They passed by a rock formation called Phantom Ship. It resembles a sailing ship seen at a distance—and it seems to disappear as it blends into background cliffs.

Vijaya Prisk, 11, of Watsonville, especially enjoyed seeing an uprooted tree called the Old Man of the Lake. "You could look a hundred feet down and see the tree standing up in the lake, all the way down at the bottom," says Vijaya. Crater Lake's exceptionally clear waters make such views possible.

Each day the backpackers set up camp before sundown. Gathering around the campfire gave them a chance to share the day's experiences. "I liked sitting around the campfire and feeling warm," Corrina recalls. "I liked looking up at the stars."

The backpackers were always careful to leave their campsites in better condition than they found them. "It's important to use good wilderness manners and to learn what benefits the environment." says Richardson. "Global resources belong to everyone."

7 | Wet and Wild In the GRAND CANYON

Shooting through rapids that jar the boat and blur the action, adventurers descend the roaring Colorado River. The river lies at the bottom of the mile-deep Grand Canyon, in Arizona. The canyon, one of the world's most spectacular places, slices through two billion years of geologic history.

DEWITT JONES

GRAND CANYON
NATIONAL PARK

'The one great sight all . . . should see'

Every year millions of visitors heed those words of President Theodore Roosevelt. Here the sun sets at Toroweap, a cliff-top overlook of the Grand Canyon. The river, scientists say, began cutting the gorge about five million years ago.

Trailblazer

John Wesley Powell (right), who later helped found the National Geographic Society, was the first to map the canyon.

'We have an unknown distance yet to run, an unknown river to explore.'

—John Wesley Powell, 1869

"We've always been a family that likes to go camping, especially out West," says Susan Thompson, of Atlanta, Georgia. Usually the family went on car camping expeditions. Though fun, they weren't always exciting. "As soon as the children became old enough to appreciate a really adventurous outing," Mrs. Thompson continues, "we wanted to give them an experience they'd never forget."

What more lasting memory could one hope for than that of a rafting trip over the roaring rapids of the Colorado River as it plows through the depths of Arizona's Grand Canyon?

But were the children old enough? Sarah, at 11, was the oldest. Following her were Martha, 10, and Lowell, 8. When their mother started calling boating outfitters, she found that most were reluctant to take children under 12.

Finally she got in touch with Richard McCallum, of Expeditions, Inc. Some 20 years before, McCallum had begun arranging river trips that included children. His first aim was to make the voyage through the canyon an adventure. He also wanted it to be a learning experience in which parents and youngsters alike would uncover the canyon's secrets of history, geology, and ecology.

Geologically, the secrets go back about two billion years. Human activity in the canyon began, by contrast, much closer to yesterday. The first humans entered the canyon perhaps 4,000 years ago. They were Indians, and they found a home amid the canyon's rugged, awesome beauty. The Indians numbered in the thousands. Today, the canyon receives three and a half million visitors a year.

The visitors owe much to a one-armed explorer named John Wesley Powell. Powell (left) was a former Union officer in the Civil War, in which he lost an arm. Both before the war and after, America was moving westward—to gold, new lands, new opportunities. But one region lay largely unexplored: the Grand Canyon. In 1869, Major Powell (as he still

Fine beaches of Arizona

At a campsite along the Colorado, teenagers build a sand castle while awaiting dinner. They are, from the left, Amanda Peet, of New York City; Raven Schwartz, of Penn Valley, Pennsylvania; and Tasha Devnani, of Safety Harbor, Florida. "We ate tacos that night," says Tasha. The beach, one of hundreds along the river, was "nice and flat," she notes.

liked to be called) led an expedition to the canyon.

Powell and his party are credited with being the first to navigate the Colorado River through the Grand Canyon. They ran one rapid after another, tasting the river's fury. "[The boat] leaps and bounds like a thing of life," Powell wrote, "and we have a wild, exhilarating ride. . . . The excitement is so great that we forget the danger until we hear the roar of a great fall below."

Powell observed Indian life in the region. He studied the area's geology. He took careful notes of the river's course. It was Major Powell, you could say, who put the Grand Canyon on the map.

Almost all Grand Canyon river trips begin at Lees Ferry, the only place within hundreds of miles where land vehicles can drive to the water's edge. Lees Ferry is mile zero on the Colorado, with all mileages both upstream and downstream being tabulated from there.

At Lees Ferry the Thompsons met their fellow voyagers. They also got acquainted with the boats. There were five of them, 18-foot river runners called Rogue Inflatables, Colorado Model. Made of rubber, the boats are sturdy and smash-resistant. The guide in each boat uses one set of oars for propelling the boat in quiet water and for steering it in

Protection for a favorite shelter

Redwall Cavern, a huge open-face cave, has sheltered probably every boating expedition that ever passed by. The cavern and the walls facing it occur in a layer of limestone. This type of rock provides much of the Grand Canyon's natural beauty. The park prohibits overnight camping here and otherwise guards against the public's "loving the canyon to death."

Canyon-style combat

When the air temperature reaches 107°F and the water is a cold 52°, river rats do the natural thing— start a water fight! In the desert air here at the bottom of the canyon, clothing dries out in minutes.

Oasis in the desert

At a place called Vasey's Paradise, water tumbles from a limestone formation, creating a lush, almost tropical fairyland. Here, Amanda and Raven refresh themselves in the falls.

rough stretches. The guide faces forward to see what's coming. That's the opposite of rowboat technique, in which the oarsman faces backward.

As the group pushed off, Martha and Lowell offered to row through the calm water that first greeted them. "It didn't look very hard, but it was," says Martha. "You had to use all your strength. I think the guides could row more easily because they were stronger."

When the boats approached rapids, the guides took over. "You can always hear the roar of roiled water before you can see the rapids themselves," says guide Carol Fritzinger. "That roar is the signal to get ready for action."

The first set of rapids came not long after the party shoved off. The water turned glassy smooth and slid down chutes over hidden rocks. Then it broke into spray and rose in almost vertical standing waves in the runout, where the water discharges from the chutes.

Skillfully guided by the oarsmen, the boats raced through the rapids. They hit lines of "haystacks"—standing waves formed where water rushing from several directions meets. The boats climbed the stacks, riding up and over in one quick motion. The shouts of the soaked passengers were lost in the roar of the waters. So ear-filling was the roar that it continued to echo through the adventurers' heads as they lay in their sleeping bags that night.

Before sundown every evening, the rafters would pull off the river to make camp. They'd lay out their sleeping bags, light the charcoal stove, and cook dinner. The river may not have changed much from the days of Major Powell, but the food has. Powell had to make do with the likes of flour, coffee, spoiled bacon, and dried apples. "We had a variety of good food," says Sarah Evans, 13, of Washington Grove, Maryland. "There were tacos, enchiladas, steaks, spaghetti, and cake."

The group would rise early each morning—some earlier than others. "Once, some people

'Crystal, here we come!'

Sarah Thompson bites her lip and closes her eyes as river guide Carol Fritzinger steers into Crystal Rapids, one of the Colorado River's wildest spots. Misjudging a wicked wave, Fritzinger lost control. The boat struck the canyon wall and tossed Sarah into *the cold and furious water. The swift current carried her downriver. Sarah washed up on some rocks in midstream, where she shivered until being rescued. Such mishaps, though infrequent, show the importance of wearing life jackets on the river.*

A hug for warmth and comfort

Fritzinger greets a bundled-up Sarah after their wet adventure. The current carried Sarah safely around rocks. It was the water's chill that posed the most danger. Too long a dunking could have led to hypothermia, loss of body heat. It can be fatal.

placed their sleeping bags too close to the river," says Sarah. "Rising water woke them up!" After a breakfast of bacon and eggs or pancakes, the rafters would set out on the river.

And so it went for 12 days. Each day was a new adventure. Each bend in the river brought new sights, the promise of discovery and excitement. On the eighth day, Sarah Thompson was reminded of the dangers faced by Major Powell and his group. At the oars, guide Fritzinger chose to take a challenging route through roaring Crystal Rapids. But she underestimated a powerful wave. The raging water banged the boat against the canyon wall. Sarah found herself suddenly in the water, borne swiftly downstream in her life jacket.

"The water felt about a million degrees below zero," Sarah recalls. "I remember bobbing up and down like a cork through waves crashing over me. I couldn't breathe very well. Eventually I washed up

Cruisin' down the river

Rubber boats drift lazily along a quiet stretch of the Colorado (left). Here, at Granite Narrows, the river is at its narrowest point in the Grand Canyon. It measures only 76 feet across.

Change of pace at mile 148

Resembling a layer cake sliced with a crooked knife, Matkatamiba Canyon (right) is a winding wonder for the boat group to explore. At the bottom runs a small stream. Over thousands of years it has carved the canyon out of limestone.

AT A GLANCE . . .

One of the seven natural wonders of the world, the Grand Canyon beckons three and a half million visitors a year. Half the park—the South Rim—is open year-round. The North Rim, which has a more severe climate, welcomes visitors from May through October.

When you visit the park, be sure to bring clothes appropriate to the season. Wear a hat to protect you from direct sunlight in summer and to retain body heat in winter. Good footgear is vital. Wear sturdy shoes or, better, hiking boots that are well broken in.

If you had wings, you'd have to travel only 18 miles to span the distance between the North and South Rims at the widest part of the canyon. By road, however, you'd have to travel 215 miles to get from one rim to the other.

On the South Rim, you can ride a mule into the canyon itself, or you can hike down. The trips last at least a full day, sometimes overnight. Half-day trips are available on the North Rim. About 20 operators offer river trips on various types of craft. The longest lasts three weeks.

For more information write—
Superintendent, Grand Canyon National Park, Grand Canyon, AZ   86023

on some rocks. One of the boatmen saw me and came out to pull me aboard."

Though the mighty Colorado can still show you very quickly who's boss, some of the danger has been erased. The inflatable rubber boats are tougher and safer than the fragile wooden craft that carried Powell and his men. Parties are led by knowledgeable guides who know how to "read the water." The National Park Service exercises care and judgment in licensing rafting companies.

Few visitors see as much of the canyon as do those who go through it by boat. The towering walls on either side are an open book of geology. The canyon slices through much of the geologic history of this part of the planet. One day well into the trip, Fritzinger pointed out that the walls were black granite, not the red limestone that they had been seeing all along. "At one time, close to two billion years ago, those rocks were the roots of mountains higher than the Rockies," she said.

"Then the mountains wore down through the action of weather and running water," she continued. "Hard as it may be to believe, a shallow sea then covered this area. Silt washed into the sea, forming layers of sand, mud, and lime. The layers

Row, row, row your boat . . .

Lowell Thompson, 8 (above, on the left), and his sister Martha, 10, discover that handling one of the river boats is not so easy as it looks. "You have to use all your strength to pull," says Martha. Below: At trip's end, Martha and Lowell help deflate the boats. The rubber craft will be folded and trucked back to the starting point 372 miles upriver.

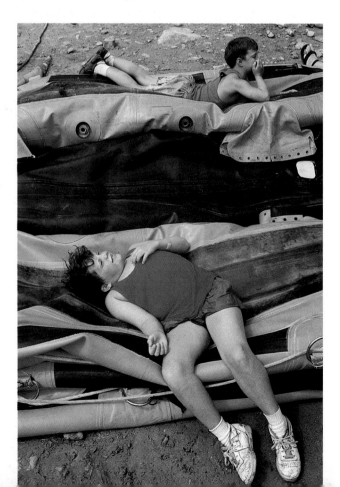

The peaceful beauty of Havasu Creek

Miles before it flows into the Colorado, Havasu Creek makes a quiet scene of graceful falls and terraced pools. Havasupai Indians have long enjoyed the mineral-tinted creek. It's now a popular side trip for visitors to the Grand Canyon.

KATHLEEN NORRIS COOK

became compressed into rock: sandstone, shale, and limestone."

About a billion years ago, pressure from inside the earth pushed the rock surfaces upward and split them into blocks. Another mountain range was thrust up, only to be eroded with time. More cycles followed. Seas gave way to swamps, which gave way to deserts. Each in turn left layers of lime, shale, and sand.

Again the land rose. It formed what today is the Colorado Plateau. Streams began flowing across the plateau about five million years ago. ("That's just a blink of the eye, in geologic terms," the guide noted.) The streams merged into what is now the Colorado River. It began cutting through the final layers—and the Grand Canyon was born. "By now," Fritzinger concluded, "the river has worn down into the granite roots of that first range."

At its deepest, the Grand Canyon measures one mile from rim to river. It holds four different life zones. Hikers going into its depths experience the same climatic and scenic changes that they would if walking from Canada to Mexico.

In the canyon's Canadian Zone, on the North Rim, the air is crisp and cool. Fir trees and aspens grow. Mule deer and wild turkeys live here. Downward, in the Transition Zone and in the Upper Sonoran Zone, the air becomes warmer and drier. Plant and animal life reflects the changing climate. At the bottom lies the Lower Sonoran Zone. It is a desert. The air broils the unprotected skin. This is the home of mesquite trees and cactuses, of rattlesnakes, skunks, and scorpions.

It was in this zone that the Thompsons' river trip began and ended. The *trip* ended, but not the thrill. That lives on in the memory of each family member—a once-in-a-lifetime adventure to be called back and enjoyed time after time. "All these things to see and discover and learn about . . . ," says Sarah. ". . . shooting down the rapids through two billion years of history. What a great vacation!"

INDEX

Bold type refers to illustrations; regular type refers to text

ADDITIONAL READING

Readers may want to check the *National Geographic Index* or a public library for related articles and to refer to the following books. ("A" indicates a book for readers at the adult level.)

Carter, Luther J., *The Florida Experience,* Johns Hopkins, 1975 (A). Clary, David A., *The Place Where Hell Bubbled Up: A History of the First National Park,* National Park Service, 1972 (A). Dickerson, Laura D., *Everglades National Park: Wonderland for Boys and Girls,* Dickson's Inc., 1970. Douglas, Marjorie Stoneman, *The Everglades: A River of Grass,* Mockingbird, 1975. Franklin, Jacque, *Where Do I Look?,* Grand Canyon Natural History Association, 1983.

Fritz, Jean, *Back to Early Cape Cod,* National Park Service, 1979. Geerlings, Paul F., *Down the Grand Staircase: Grand Canyon's Living Adventure,* Grand Canyon Publications, 1981 (A). Hughes, Donald J., *In the House of Stone and Light,* Grand Canyon Natural History Association, 1985 (A). Kaye, Glen, *Cape Cod: The Story Behind the Scenery,* KC Publications, 1980. Lavender, David, *River Runners of the Grand Canyon,* University of Arizona Press, 1985 (A).

Leaden, Tim, *The West Coast Trail and Nitinat Lakes,* Douglas & McIntyre (Vancouver/Toronto), 1987 (A). Spring, Bob, and Ira Spring, *Crater Lake National Park,* Superior, 1978. Stephenson, Marylee, *Canada's National Parks: A Visitor's Guide,* Prentice–Hall, 1984. Will, Robin, *Beautiful Yosemite National Park,* Beautiful America Publishing, 1983. Williams, Howell, *Crater Lake: The Story of Its Origin,* University of California, 1972 (A).

BOOKS BY THE NATIONAL GEOGRAPHIC SOCIETY: *America's Wonderlands,* 1980 (A). *Natural Wonders of North America,* 1984. *Our Threatened Inheritance* (with companion handbook, *Our Federal Lands*), 1984 (A). *Wilderness Challenge,* 1980. *Yellowstone Country: An Enduring Wonder,* 1989 (A).

CONSULTANTS

Nicholas J. Long, Ph.D., *Consulting Psychologist*
Frank J. Sanford, *Reading Consultant*

The Special Publications and School Services Division is grateful to the individuals named or quoted within the text and to those cited here for their generous assistance:

G. Frank Ackerman, Cape Cod National Seashore; Pam Baird, Ucluelet Recreation Commission; Myrna Boulding, Strathcona Park Lodge; Bruce Brossman, Yosemite Mountaineering School; Barry Campbell, Howie F. Hambleton, and Bill McIntyre, Pacific Rim National Park.

Lisa Dapprich and John Poimiroo, Yosemite National Park; Sandy Dayhoff, Dave Kronk, and Pat Tolle, Everglades National Park; Jack DeGolia, Steven Fuller, and Roderick Hutchinson, Yellowstone National Park; Bernard Hurns, Miami Shores Elementary School.

Richard and Susie McCallum, Expeditions, Inc.; Helen McCoy, Westview Elementary School (Miami); Linda Meyers, Harpers Ferry Center; Craig Richardson; Connie Rudd, Grand Canyon National Park; Vivian Williams, Parks Canada.

ILLUSTRATIONS CREDITS

Susan Sanford, MedSciArtCo (2, 8, 24, 39, 51, 60, 67 symbol, 75 symbol, 76 inset map, 82); U.S. Department of the Interior, National Park Service (arrowhead symbol, throughout); courtesy National Park Service, artist Robert E. Hynes (14); Yellowstone National Park (16); Florida National Parks and Monuments Association, Inc. (32); Peter B. Gallagher (33); John Poimiroo (42); Yosemite Park and Curry Company (44); Cape Cod National Seashore (55); Environment Canada, Parks (69); courtesy National Park Service, artist Jaime Quintero (76-77); Grand Canyon National History Association (91).

Library of Congress CIP Data

Adventures in your national parks.
(Books for world explorers)
Bibliography: p.
Includes index.
Summary: Provides an introduction to the national parks of the United States and Canada through the adventures of various young people as they explore Yellowstone, Yosemite, the Everglades, Cape Cod, Pacific Rim, Crater Lake, and Grand Canyon.
1. National parks and reserves—United States—Juvenile literature. 2. United States—Description and travel—1981- —Juvenile literature. [1. National parks and reserves] I. Series.
E160.A32 1988   353.0086'35   88-31473
ISBN 0-87044-702-5
ISBN 0-87044-707-6 (lib. bdg.)

Composition for ADVENTURES IN YOUR NATIONAL PARKS by the Typographic section of National Geographic Production Services, Pre-Press Division. Type mechanicals by Carrie A. Edwards. Printed and bound by Arcata Graphics, Kingsport, Tenn. Film preparation by Catharine Cooke Studio, Inc., New York, N.Y. Color separations by Lanman-Progressive Co., Washington, D.C.; Lincoln Graphics, Inc., Cherry Hill, N.J.; and NEC, Inc., Nashville, Tenn. Cover printed by Federated Lithographers-Printers, Inc., Providence, R.I. Teacher's Guide printed by McCollum Press, Inc., Rockville, Md.

ADVENTURES IN YOUR NATIONAL PARKS

PUBLISHED BY
THE NATIONAL GEOGRAPHIC SOCIETY
WASHINGTON, D. C.

Gilbert M. Grosvenor, *President and Chairman of the Board*
Melvin M. Payne, Thomas W. McKnew, *Chairmen Emeritus*
Owen R. Anderson, *Executive Vice President*
Robert L. Breeden, *Senior Vice President, Publications and Educational Media*

PREPARED BY THE SPECIAL PUBLICATIONS AND SCHOOL SERVICES DIVISION
Donald J. Crump, *Director*
Philip B. Silcott, *Associate Director*
Bonnie S. Lawrence, *Assistant Director*

BOOKS FOR WORLD EXPLORERS
Pat Robbins, *Editor*
Ralph Gray, *Editor Emeritus*
Ursula Perrin Vosseler, *Art Director*
Margaret McKelway, *Associate Editor*
Larry Nighswander, *Illustrations Editor*

STAFF FOR *ADVENTURES IN YOUR NATIONAL PARKS*
Ross Bankson, *Managing Editor*
Glover S. Johns III, *Picture Editor*
Sheila M. Green, *Senior Researcher*
Catherine D. Hughes, *Contributing Researcher*
Donald L. Carrick, *Design Assistant*
Kathryn N. Adams, Sandra F. Lotterman, *Editorial Assistants*
Janet A. Dustin, Jennie H. Proctor, *Illustrations Assistants*
D. Mark Carlson, Donald L. Carrick, Joseph F. Ochlak, Martin S. Walz, *Poster Map Research and Production*

ENGRAVING, PRINTING, AND PRODUCT MANUFACTURE: George V. White, *Director;* Vincent P. Ryan, *Manager;* David V. Showers, *Production Manager;* Lewis R. Bassford, *Production Project Manager;* Kathie Cirucci, Timothy H. Ewing, *Senior Production Assistants;* Kevin Heubusch, *Production Assistant;* Carol R. Curtis, *Senior Production Staff Assistant*

STAFF ASSISTANTS: Aimée L. Brown, Catherine G. Cruz, Marisa Farabelli, Mary Elizabeth House, Rebecca A. Hutton, Karen Katz, Lisa A. LaFuria, Eliza C. Morton, Dru Stancampiano, Nancy J. White

MARKET RESEARCH: Joseph S. Fowler, Carrla L. Holmes, Marla Lewis, Joseph Roccanova, Donna R. Schoeller, Marsha Sussman, Judy T. Guerrieri

INDEX: Elisabeth MacRae-Bobynskyj